How to Protect your Business from Burglary, Embezzlement, Employee Pilferage and Bad-Check Passers

By Meir Liraz

Published by BizMove
www.bizmove.com

ISBN: 9781090516084

Table of Contents

1. How to Prevent Embezzlement

An owner-manager can lose a great deal of money before even suspecting that embezzlement might be going on. That's because by definition this crime is committed by someone in a position of trust. The loss may involve a small amount taken by an employee from the cash register. Or a considerable sum stolen through an elaborate scheme of juggling the books.

Simple controls built into the accounting system can often forestall any such practices in your operation. In any case, the proper internal controls may help document incriminating evidence, without which it is difficult to estimate your loss for insurance purposes or even to prove that it resulted from a crime.

This preventing embezzlement Guide offers suggestions on how you can thwart dishonest practices. It also discusses what you should do if it appears that one of your employees has embezzled from your business.

You may not have has any experience with embezzlers. But many owner-managers have. Everyday there are newspaper stories about how some dishonest employee has managed to divert company funds to his or her own pocket. It happens often enough to make it worth your while to give the subject some thought and to examine your record-keeping and auditing procedures to make sure there are no tempting loopholes.

Embezzlement is "the fraudulent appropriation of property by a person to whom it has been entrusted." That's what makes this crime different from ordinary theft or larceny. The embezzler is someone in your company whom you trust.

You need to have a system of internal control to safeguard money and other property subject to embezzlement. Of course, nobody wants to run a business like an armed camp. But if you have a built-in control system, administer it tightly, and audit it frequently, you may prevent attempts of embezzlement. At any rate, you will have the means to collect evidence that may expose a crime.

Embezzlers usually think that they are clever - smarter than the owner-manager and cunning enough to beat the system. Before you set about to outwit them, it is a good idea to be familiar with some of their methods

Some Common Schemes

The embezzler is usually a trusted employee who is taking advantage of the employer's confidence. In many cases the embezzler has been given more authority than the position calls for. Methods of embezzling are limited only by imagination.

In the simplest situation, cash is received and the employee merely pockets it without making a record of the transaction. A theft of this type is difficult to prevent or detect if the transaction is a cash sale and no subsequent entry is necessary in receipt or accounts receivable records. To reduce temptation, prenumbered sales invoices or cash receipts should be used for all sales regardless of the amount. Spot checks and other monitoring procedures can also help assure you that cash sales are actually being recorded.

A somewhat more complicated type of embezzlement is called lapping. This involves the temporary withholding of receipts such as payments on accounts receivable. Lapping is a continuing scheme which usually starts with a small amount but can run into thousands of dollars before it is detected. For example, take an employee who opens mail or otherwise receives cash and checks as payment on open accounts. The employee holds out a $100 dollar cash payment made by customer "A" on March 1. To avoid arousing suspicion on "A's" part, $100 is then taken from a $200 payment made by customer "B" on March 4. This is sent on, together with the necessary documentation, for processing and crediting to the account of "A." The embezzler pockets the remaining $100, which increases the shortage to $200.

As this "borrowing" procedure continues, the employee makes away with increasingly larger amounts of money involving more and more accounts. A fraud of this nature can run on for years. Of course, it requires detailed record-keeping by the embezzler in order to keep track of the shortage and transfer it from one account to another to avoid suspicion. Any indication that an employee is keeping personal records of business transactions outside your regular books of account should be looked into.

Sometimes an embezzler who is carrying on a lapping scheme also has access to accounts receivable records and statements. In this case, he or she is in a position to alter the statements mailed out to customers. Thus the fraud may continue undetected over a long period of time, until something unusual happens. A customer complaint may spotlight the situation. Or the matter may be surfaced through audit procedures such as confirmation of accounts receivable. One embezzler who also handled the customer complaints was able to avoid detection for many years. The amount of shortage reached such proportions and covered so many accounts that he dared not take a vacation. He even ate lunch at his desk lest some other employee receive an inquiry from a customer concerning a discrepancy in a statement. The owner-manager for whom he worked admired his diligence and loyalty. Fellow workers marveled that his apparent frugality enable him to enjoy a rather high standard of living. But the inevitable finally happened. this employee was hospitalized with a serious ailment, and in his absence his fraudulent scheme came to light. One reason many firms require regular vacations is to keep some "indispensable man" from dispensing with company funds illegally.

Sometimes company bank accounts are used for check-kiting. In fact, losses from some large check-kiting schemes have been great enough to cause a company to go broke.

In the usual scheme, the check-kiter must be in the position to write checks on and make deposits in two or more bank accounts. One account could be the embezzler's personal account and the other a business checking account. If the embezzler has an accomplice in another business, two business accounts may be used. If your company has more than one checking account at different banks, these accounts may be utilized to carry out the fraud.

The check-kiter is taking advantage of the time period (or "float") which is the number of days between deposit of a check and collection of funds. There may be several days between the date when a kited check drawn on bank "A" is deposited in bank "B" and the date the check is presented to the bank

"A" for payment. Assuming that it takes 3 business days for checks to clear, a simple kite between two banks could be accomplished as follows:

On December 1, a check in the amount of $5,000 drawn on bank "A" is deposited in bank "B." On December 2, the check-kiter cashes a $5,000 check payable to cash and drawn on bank "B" with a teller at bank "B." Since the original kited check will be presented to bank "A" on December 4, the check kiter on or before that date will deposit a $6,000 check drawn on bank "B" in bank "A" not only to insure payment of the original kited check but to increase the amount of the kite. As the process is repeated the kited checks become larger, more cash is withdrawn, and the scheme can continue until the shortage is covered - or until the kite "breaks" when one of the banks refuses to honor a kited check because the funds on deposit are uncollected.

A temporary kite may be used by a dishonest employee to conceal cash shortage at the end of a period by depositing a kited check into your company account. This brings the bank balance into agreement with the books. CPAs will request "cut-off" bank statements to detect frauds of this type.

Payroll frauds are yet another source of loss to management. Occasionally an enterprising embezzler has added the names of relatives or fictitious individuals to the company payroll and thus enjoyed several salary checks each week instead of one.

Sometimes, when a company becomes large enough that the owner-manager can no longer exercise personal surveillance of accounting activities, opportunities arise for a dishonest employee to set up a dummy supplier and falsify documentation of fictitious purchase transactions.

Dishonest employees can figure out any number of ways to defraud their employers. Purchasing agents can accept "kickbacks" from suppliers from purchasing goods at inflated prices. Salespeople and others can pad their expense accounts. Personal items can sometimes be bought and charged to the company. Cashiers in retail firms can undercharge relatives or friends for merchandise. False vouchers can be prepared to conceal thefts from petty cash funds. Overtime can be falsely recorded. Moreover, quite substantial amounts of money may be lost through the cumulative effect of such seemingly minor abuses as personal use of company postage stamps, supplies, and equipment, as well as charging personal long-distance phone calls to the business. And so on.

Make Your System Fraud-Proof

The first and one of the most important things an owner-manager should do is to set a good example.

Your employees watch what you do and are prone to imitate your habits - good or bad. An employer who dips into petty cash, fudges on an expense account, uses company funds for personal items, or sets other examples of loose business behavior will find employees rationalizing dishonest actions with the attitude "if it's good enough for the boss, its good enough for me."

Another important way an owner-manager can discourage embezzlement is by establishing a climate of accountability. Employees should know their jobs and feel trusted. But they should also realize that they are held accountable for their actions. To some people, management indifference in financial administration is a license to steal. That's why it is important for you to examine your procedures and determine what controls can be added to forestall any dishonest practices. And, just as important, the system should be designed to help document evidence in the event someone does try to embezzle your funds. One problem in fidelity loss claims is that of proving the amount that was stolen. The owner-manager has to support a loss claim with evidence - facts and figures that you get from your records.

Reliance for prevention and detection of fraud must be placed principally upon an adequate accounting system with appropriate internal controls that safeguard your assets. Your public accountant can be of great help in setting up a good record-keeping system. Then it must be tested and evaluated at least annually by the auditor. The purpose of periodic examination is to make sure that there are no loopholes through which an embezzler can manipulate your funds.

One fundamental control is separation of the duties of employees. For example, persons concerned with receiving checks and cash should not also be responsible for the entries in the accounts receivable records. No one person should handle a transaction from beginning to end. If you do not exercise tight control over invoices, purchase orders, discounts, customer credits, and so forth, you are asking for trouble.

You should insist that your accounting system provide you with operating statements issued at least monthly. These will inform you of the operations to date and the firm's financial condition. You can use these documents to compare the figures with prior periods. Any unusual or unexplained variations should be discussed with your public accountant to determine the reason.

Look For Clues

You know how in medicine the symptoms of one disease often resemble those of another. Likewise in business the symptoms, or danger signs, of an embezzlement are often caused by other factors. Here are a few clues which indicate that either an embezzler is at work in your company or certain aspects of the business need more of your attention.

Increase in overall sales returns could be caused by defective merchandise - or it might represent a concealment of accounts receivable payments.

Unusual bed-debt write-offs can be due to a number of business reasons - or they could be covering up a fraudulent scheme.

A decline or usually small increase in cash or credit sales might mean that business has not been good - or it could mean that some sales were not being recorded.

Inventory shortage can be caused by error or mismanagement - or they could indicate fictitious purchases, unrecorded sales, or employee pilferage.

Profit declines and/or increases in expenses can be entirely legitimate - or they could be a sign that cash is being siphoned off illegitimately.

Slow collections can be caused by business conditions - or they can be a device to mask an embezzlement.

Ounces Of Prevention

There are many steps an owner-manager can take to cut down on the possibility of losses through embezzlement. Do you take the following precautions?

1. Check the background of prospective employees. Sometimes you can satisfy yourself by making a few telephone calls or writing a few letters. In other cases, you may want to turn the matter over to a credit bureau or similar agency to run a background check. (Keep in mind that the rights of individuals must be preserved in furnishing, receiving, and using background information).

2. Know your employees to the extent that you may be able to detect signs of financial or personal problems. Build up rapport so that they feel free to discuss such things with you in confidence.

3. See that no one is placed on the payroll without authorization from you or a responsible official of the company. If you have a personnel department, require that it approve additions to the payroll as a double check.

4. Have the company mail addressed to a post office box rather than to your place of business. In smaller cities, the owner-manager may want to go to the post office to collect the mail. In any event, you or your designated key person should personally

open the mail and make a record at that time of cash and checks received. Don't delude yourself that checks or money orders payable to your company can't be converted into cash by an enterprising embezzler.

5. Either personally prepare the daily cash deposits or compare the deposits made by employees with the record of cash and checks received. Make sure you get a copy of the duplicate deposit slip or other documentation from the bank. Make it a habit to go to the bank and make the daily deposit yourself as often as you can. If you delegate these jobs, make an occasional spot check to see that nothing is amiss.

6. Arrange for bank statements and other correspondence from banks to be sent to the same post office box, and personally reconcile all bank statements with your company's books and records. The owner-manager who has not reconciled the statements for some time may want to get orientated by the firm's outside accountant.

7. Personally examine all canceled checks and endorsements to see if there is anything unusual. This also applies to payroll checks.

8. Make sure that an employee in a position to mishandle funds is adequately bonded. Let employees know that fidelity coverage is a matter of

company policy rather that any feeling of mistrust on your part. If would-be embezzlers know that a bonding company also has an interest in what they do, they may think twice before helping themselves to your funds.

9. Spot check your accounting records and assets to satisfy yourself that all is well and that your plan of internal control is being carried out.

10. Personally approve unusual discounts and bad-debt write-offs. Approve or spot check credit memos and other documentation for sales returns and allowances.

11. Don't delegate the signing of checks and approval of cash disbursements unless absolutely necessary and never approve any payment without sufficient documentation or prior knowledge of the transaction.

12. Examine all invoices and supporting data before signing checks. Make sure that all merchandise was actually received and the price seems reasonable. In many false purchase schemes, the embezzler neglects to make up receiving forms or other records purporting to show receipt of merchandise.

13. Personally cancel all invoices at the time you sign the check to prevent double payment through error or otherwise.

14. Don't sign blank checks. Don't leave a supply of signed blank checks when you go on vacation.

15. Inspect all prenumbered checkbooks and other prenumbered forms from time to time to insure that checks or forms from the backs of the books have not been removed and possibly used in a fraudulent scheme.

16. Have the preparation of the payroll and the actual paying of employees handled by different persons, especially when cash is involved.

If You Suspect A Crime

First of all, be sure that you do not jump to any unwarranted conclusions. What may appear to be an obvious embezzlement may, on further investigation, turn out to have a perfectly valid explanation. A false accusation could result in serious civil liability. There have been cases where employees have been charged by management with embezzlement, dismissed from their positions, and later found to be entirely innocent.

But if you have good reason to suspect embezzling, contact your attorney immediately. Be guided by legal advice on how to proceed. Discuss the necessity of notifying the bonding company and appropriate law enforcement authorities. follow legal advice in matters regarding prosecution so that you will not subject yourself or your company to charges of false arrest.

Don't subject yourself to criminal charges by helping to conceal the commission of a crime. Embezzlers should be prosecuted when the facts so warrant and when there is a sufficiency of evidence. These and other legal questions are best left to your attorney.

Computer-Related Embezzlements

The news media have given a lot of publicity to computer-assisted frauds and embezzlements. The computer crimes receiving this publicity are usually complex and give the impression that computers-related frauds can be committed only by highly skilled technicians using sophisticated computer systems. This could create a feeling of false security for owner-managers who use less sophisticated systems or service centers for processing their records.

A study by the U.S. General Accounting Office of Computer-Related Crimes in Federal Programs disclosed that most computer-related crimes were committed by people with limited knowledge of computer technology. Most cases resulted from preparation of false input data to computer-based systems. Neglect of control on input is a weakness.

You should have your outside accountant review your controls and strengthen it if needed.

To Sum Up

There are three principal ways in which you can minimize the possibility of embezzlement losses. None is completely effective without the others.

Internal controls are perhaps the most effective safeguard against fraud, but even the best precautions can't make it absolutely impossible.

Independent audits discourage fraud and may uncover it. but they can't, as some people mistakenly believe, guarantee disclosure of all irregularities.

Fidelity coverage can help you recover what may be lost in spite of your best efforts to prevent embezzlements.

2. How to Prevent Burglary And Robbery Loss

Stores are prime targets for burglars and robbers. Seeking dark and easy-to-enter stores, burglars usually operate at night. Attracted by careless displays of cash, robbers often strike at opening or closing time or when customer traffic is light.

Because you may be the next victim of a robbery or a burglary in your area, you should be aware of the precautionary measures that are available to lessen the impact of these two crimes.

Burglary

Burglary is any unlawful entry to commit a felony or a theft, even though no force was used to gain entrance.

Retailers whose stores have been broken into know that burglaries are costly. What these business owners may not be aware of is that the number of burglaries has doubled in the past several years and, therefore, they may be two-, three-, or four-time losers if the trend is not reversed.

Moreover, few burglars are caught. Almost 80 percent of all burglaries go unsolved. Police prevention and detection are difficult because of lack of witnesses or evidence to identify the criminal.

Burglary prevention must start with the small merchant - you. You can use a combination of measures to protect your store from burglars. Among the things you can use are: 1) suitable locks, (2) an appropriate alarm system, (3) adequate indoor and outside lighting, and (4) a secure store safe.

In addition, the owners of high-risk stores - ones in areas with a reputation for rampant crime-should also consider using: (1) heavy window screens, (2) burglar resistant glass windows, (3) private police patrols, and (4) watchdogs.

Locks. Be sure to use the right kind of lock on your doors. In addition to being an obstacle to unwanted entry, a strong lock requires a burglar to use force to get into the store. Under standard burglary insurance policies, evidence of a forced entry is necessary to collect on burglary insurance.

Most experts on locks agree that the pin-tumbler cylinder lock provides the best security. It may have from 3 to 7 pins. Locksmiths caution, however, that a burglar can easily pick a lock with less than 5 pins.

(There are a few non-pin tumbler locks that give high security, but you should check with a locksmith before you use one.)

Dead bolt locks should be used. They cannot be opened by sliding a piece of flexible material between the door edge and door jamb. (Dead bolt is a lock bolt that is moved positively by turning the knob or key without action of a spring.)

When you use a double cylinder dead lock, the door cannot be opened without a key on either side. This fact means that on a glass door there is no handle for a burglar to reach by merely breaking the glass. Such a lock also provides protection against "break-outs" - a thief being concealed before closing time and breaking out with stolen goods.

Safeguarding entrance ways, especially the rear door, cannot be over emphasized. Bar the rear door, in addition to locking it, because many burglars favor back doors.

Installing Locks. The best lock is ineffective if it is not properly installed. For example, if a lock with a 5/8" long latch blot is installed in a door that is separated from the door-jamb by 1/2", the effective length of the bolt is cut to only 1/8". Have a locksmith check the locks on your exterior doors to be sure that your locks give you the right protection.

Key Control. To keep keys from falling into the hands of burglars, issue as few keys as possible. Keep a record on the keys you issue. Exercise the same care with keys as you would a thousand dollar bill. Do the following:

1. Avoid the danger of key duplication. Caution employees not the leave store keys with parking lot attendants, or in a topcoat hanging in a restaurant, or lying about the office or stockroom.

2. Keep your records on key distribution up-to-date so that you know what keys have been issued to whom.

3. Whenever a key is lost or an employee leaves the firm, without turning in his or her key, re-key your store.

4. Take special care to protect the "master key" used to remove cylinders from locks.

5. Have one key and lock for outside doors and a different key and lock for your office. Don't master-key because it weakens your security.

6. Have a code for each key so that it does not have to be visibly tagged and only an authorized person can know the specific lock that key fits. Don't use a key chain with a tag carrying the store's address.

7. Take a periodic inventory of keys. Have employees show you each key so you will know it has not been lost, mislaid, or loaned.

Burglar Alarms. The silent central-station burglary alarm system gives your store the best protection. The reason: It does not notify the burglar as does the local alarm-such as a siren or bell-outside the store. A silent alarm alerts only the specialists who know how to handle burglaries.

In large cities, central alarm systems are available on a rental basis from private firms in this business; in small cities, they are often tied directly into police headquarters. Part of the cost for installing a silent alarm system will sometimes be defrayed by a reduction in your burglary insurance premium.

Although a building-type local alarm is cheaper and easier to install, it too often only warns the thief and is not considered by specialists to be as effective as a central station alarm. Of course, if no central alarm service system is available, or such an alarm is not economically feasible, then by all means install a building alarm.

Whether your alarm is central or local, you have a wide choice of alarm sensing devices. Among them are radar motion detectors, invisible photo beams, detectors that work on ultrasonic sound, and vibration detectors. Also there is supplemental equipment, such as an automatic phone dialer. This phones the police and the store owner, and gives then verbal warning when an alarm is breached.

Each type of alarm has advantages in certain situations. For example, proximity alarms are often used on safe cabinets. You should seek professional guidance to get the best alarm for your needs.

Flood Your Store With Lights. Outdoor lighting is another way to shield the store from burglary. Almost all store break-ins occur at night. Darkness conceals the burglar and gives him or her time to work.

By floodlighting the outside of your store on all sides you can defeat many burglars. All sides include alley entrances and side passageways between buildings where entry might be made.

Mercury and metallic vapor lamps are good for illuminating the exterior walls of a store. They are designed to withstand vandalism and weather-wind velocities up to 100 miles per hour. Some have a heat tempered lens that cannot be broken with less than a 22 caliber rifle.

Indoor lighting is also important. When a store is lighted inside, police officers can see persons in the store or notice the disorder which burglars usually cause. When the store is left dark, a burglar can see the police approaching, but they can't see the burglar.

Police get to know the lighted stores and will check the premises when, and if, the light is off.

It is also important to arrange window displays so police patrols can see into the store.

Your Safe. Be sure the safe in which you keep your money and other valuables is strong enough to deter burglars. Police remind merchants that a file cabinet with a combination lock is not a money safe. Store money should be protected in a Burglar-resistant Money Chest -as such safes are properly called.

Insurance companies recognize the E Safe as adequate for most merchant risks (except, in a few cities, where torch and explosive attacks on safes are common). Insurance companies give a sizable reduction in premiums for use of the E Safe. Over the years, the saving can pay the added cost of an E Safe.

Locating Your Safe. Putting a safe in the back of the store or where it is not visible from the street, invites burglary. Police recommend that the safe be visible to the outside street. Also the safe area should be well lighted all night.

But visibility and lighting will be wasted effort if your safe can be carted off by a burglar. Weight is no guarantee that the safe can't be stolen. Safes weighing 2,000 pounds have been taken out of stores.

No matter what the safe weighs, bolt it to the building structure.

Leave The "Cupboard Bare." Even when you use an "E" rated burglar-resistant money box, it is a good idea to keep on hand the barest minimum of cash. Bank all excess cash each day.

Leave your cash register drawer empty and open at night. A burglar will break into a closed one, and the damage to your register can be costly.

In addition to leaving the "cupboard" as bare as possible, use a silent central station alarm on your safe cabinet. When closing your safe at night, be sure to do the following:

1. Check to see that everything has been put into the safe.

2. Make a note of the serial numbers on large bills taken in after your daily deposit.

3. Check to be sure that your safe is locked.

4. Activate the burglar alarm.

Make it a practice never to leave the combination of your safe on store premises. Change the combination when an employee who knows it leaves your firm.

High-risk Locations. Some stores are in high-risk locations. These areas have a reputation for crime. Night after night, people break display windows and help themselves or force their way into stores.

Because many windows are smashed on impulse, you should minimize the chance of loss. If possible, remove attractive and expensive merchandise from the window at night. Many jewelry stores protect items left in the display window by secondary glass- a piece of heavy glass hanging on chains from the window's ceiling. Being non-fixed, the secondary glass is difficult to break even if the burglar smashes the display window.

If your store is in a high-risk location, you need to consider using heavy window screens, burglar-resistant glass, watch dogs, or private police patrols.

Heavy Window Screens. Heavy metal window screens or grating are an inexpensive way for protecting show windows. You store them during business hours. At closing time, you put the screens up and lock them in place.

Burglar-resistant Glass. When used in exterior doors, windows, display windows, and in interior showcases, this type of glass deters burglars. It has a high tensile strength that allows it to take considerable beating. It is useful in areas with vandalism problems.

Burglar-resistant glass is a laminated sandwich with a sheet of invisible plastic compressed between two sheets of glass. It mounts like ordinary plate glass and comes in clear, tinted, and opaque.

Of course, this type of glass can be broken with continual hammering-as with a baseball bat or sledge hammer. But it will not shatter. The burglar who is patient enough to bang a hole in the glass will find it bordered by a barrier of jagged glass icicles.

Even in prestige locations, burglar-resistant glass offers protection. It can be used in stores selling high value merchandise, such as cameras, furs, and jewelry.

Watchdogs. In larger cities, agencies offer watch dog service on a nominal hourly basis. An owner-manager can use these dogs on a spot check basis one or two night a week to deter burglars. Word soon gets around that a store is using watchdogs, and burglars cross the store off their list. The sight and sound of an angry watchdog makes them afraid.

Private Police Patrols. A private police patrol can be used to supplement the public police force when it is undermanned and overworked. A private patrol can discourage burglars by checking the store during the night. Sometimes private police may catch a burglar in the act; other times they can discover the break-in shortly after it occurs. In either case, their prompt notice to the police increases the likelihood of catching the culprit and recovering your merchandise and money.

A private patrol is also qualified to testify on the store conditions prior to a crime. This sort of testimony expedites the payment of insurance claims. In disaster, such as a flood or riot, private police can initiate emergency measures.

Private patrol can also help you train your employees, reveal unlocked doors, open windows, and other signs of employee carelessness which they can help correct.

Robbery

Robbery is stealing or taking anything of value by force, or violence, or by use of fear.

Only about one third of the robberies are solved by identification and arrest. Even when robbers are caught almost none of the cash or property is recovered.

Robbery is a violent crime. The robber always uses force or the threat of force, and the victims are often hurt. In 65 percent of store holdups, the robber uses a weapon.

What can you do to reduce losses from robbery in your store?

Your first line of defense is training your people. How you handle your cash is also important. Two other vital defense actions are: (1) you should use care in opening and closing your store and (2) you should use care when answering after-hours emergency calls.

Training to Reduce Risk. You should let each of your employees know what may happen if a robbery occurs. Train them on how to act during a holdup.

Emphasize the protection of lives as well as money. Warn each person that you want no "heroes." The heroic action by an employee or customer may end as a deadly mistake. The robber is as volatile as a bottle of nitro-glycerine. Handle him or her with the same care you would use with any explosive.

Instruct your people to the following when, and if, they face a robber:

(1) Reassure the robber that they will cooperate in every way.

(2) Stay as calm as possible.

(3) Spend their time making mental notes on the criminal's build, hair color, complexion, voice, what he or she is wearing, and anything that would make it possible to identify him or her. A calm accurate description of the robber can help bring him or her to justice. (Police advise that employees should not discuss or compare descriptions with each other but wait until the police arrive.)

You can provide a reference point to make descriptions accurate. Mark the wall or the edge of the door jamb in such a way that later the employee will be able to give a more accurate estimate of the robber's height. Often the person who has been held up compares the criminal's height with that of another person in the store. The clerk ends up unconsciously describing this innocent person used for comparison, rather than the robber.

Instruct your employees not to disclose the amount of loss. The police and news reporters should receive such information only from you. When talking to reporters, play down the theft. Don't picture your store as being an easy mark with a great deal of cash on hand.

Don't Build Up Cash. Cash on hand is the lure that attracts a robber. The best deterrent is to keep as little cash in the store as possible. Another deterrent is camera equipment that photographs robbers.

Make bank deposits daily. During selling hours, check the amount of cash in your register or registers. Remove all excess cash from each register several times a day.

Do not set up cashier operations so that they are visible to outsiders. The sight of money can trigger crime. Balance your register an hour or two before closing, not at closing time. Make it a rule to keep your safe locked even during business hours.

When making bank deposits, use an armored car service, if practical. If not, you should take a different route to the bank each day and vary the time of the deposit. Obviously, the best time to make deposits is during daylight hours.

You should also vary the routes you travel between the store and your home. Keep your store keys on a separate key ring. At least then, you won't be stranded by the loss of your car and personal keys.

Opening and Closing Routine. Opening or closing the store is a two-man job. When opening your store, station one person - an employee or your assistant - outside

where he or she can observe your actions. You enter the store, check the burglar alarm to be sure it is still properly set, then move around in the store and look for any signs of unwanted callers.

You and your assistant should have an agreement on the length of time this pre-opening check is to take. Then if you do not reappear at the scheduled time, your assistant should phone the police.

The outside person should always know where the nearest phone is located. He or she should have a card in his or her wallet with the police phone number typed on it and coins taped to the back side of the card so that he or she has the right change to make the call.

When calling the police, calmly;

1. Give his or her name.

2. Give the name and address of the store.

3. Report that a holdup is in progress at the store.

Under normal conditions, the owner-manager would return to the entrance after finishing the store inspection and give the outside person a predetermined "all clear" signal.

Your night closing should be a similar routine. A few minutes before closing, you make a routine check of stockrooms, furnace room, storeroom, and other places where a thief might hide. A second employee should wait just outside the store until you have finished your inspection. If you drive to work, he or she should bring your car to a location near the exit door. He or she should watch while you set the burglar alarm and lock the doors and windows.

Be Cautious of Night Calls. Whenever you receive an emergency call to return to the store at night, be careful.

First, never return to the store without first notifying someone that you are returning.

Second, if it is a burglar-alarm break, phone the police department and ask that a police car meet you at the store.

Third, if it is a repair problem, phone the repair company and have the service truck sent out before you leave home.

Fourth, if you arrive at the store and do not see the police car, or the repair truck, do not park near the store. And do not enter the store.

Fifth, make it a habit to verify all phone calls you receive after store hours, no matter where they originate. A careless slip on your part may be all the criminal is waiting for.

Following these precautions can mean the difference between life and death.

3. How to Prevent Employee Pilferage

Not all crooks roam the streets of the nation's cities. Many spend their time in the manufacturing plants of companies. There, disguised as honest citizens, they shoplift and pilfer whatever comes to hand, often tampering with records to cover up their thefts.

To prevent pilferage, an owner-manager must recognize that some employees cannot be trusted and make all employees aware that he or she is taking steps to thwart dishonest personnel. Such steps include setting up a system of loss prevention (devices and procedures), administering the system rigidly, and auditing it often to discourage dishonest employees who try to bypass the system.

To steal or not to steal? That is the question facing employees in plants. Many employees answer that question almost unconsciously. They see items lying around and pick them up for their own use. They slip small hand tools into their pockets. Or they dip into the bin for a fistful of nuts and bolts or snip off a few feet of wire for a home repair job.

But not all employees who pilfer are nickel-and-dime thieves. Some are professionals who carry off thousands of dollars worth of equipment and materials.

Misplaced Trust

One reason for pilferage is misplaced trust. Many owner-managers of small companies feel close to their employees. Some regard their employees as partners. These owner-managers trust their people with keys, a safe combination, cash, and records.

Thus, these employees have at hand the tools which a thief or embezzler needs for a successful crime.

Unfortunately, some of the "trusted" employees in many small businesses are larger partners than their bosses anticipate. Unless you're taking active steps to prevent loss from in-plant pilferage, some are probably trying to steal your business, little by little, right from under your nose. Few indeed are the businesses in which dishonest employees are not busily at work. Usually, these employees are protected by management's indifference or ineptitude as they steal a little, steal a lot, but nevertheless, steal first the profit, and then the business itself.

One of the first steps in preventing shoplifting and pilferage is for the owner-manager to examine the trust he or she puts in employees. Is it blind trust that grew from close friendships? Or is it trust that is built on an accountability that reduces opportunities for thefts?

A Climate for Dishonesty

In addition to misplacing trust, it is easy for an owner-manager to create an environment in which dishonesty takes root and thrives. Just relax your accounting and inventory control procedures. Nothing deters would-be thieves like the knowledge that inventory is so closely controlled that stolen goods will be missed quickly.

And what about the plant where its common practice for a close relative or two of the boss to help themselves from the stockroom without signing for the items they take? Soon such a plant becomes a place where inventory shrinkage soars as employees get the message that record keeping is loose and controls are lax.

In a manufacturing plant, no materials and no finished goods should be taken without a requisition or a removal record being made. Exceptions? Absolutely none.

Similarly, the owner-manager who does not exercise tight control over invoices, purchase orders, removals (for example, for tools, materials, and finished goods), and credits is asking for embezzlement, fraud, and unbridled theft. Crooked office workers and production and maintenance personnel dream about sloppily kept records and un-watched inventory. Why make their dreams come true?

One shipping platform employee's dream came true to the tune of $30,000 - the amount of goods he stole from his company. When caught, he said, "It was so easy, I really didn't think anyone cared."

Let people know you care. Make them aware of the stress you place on loss-prevention.

This point must be driven home again and again. And with every restatement of It - whether by a security check, a change of locks, the testing of alarms, a systems audit, a notice on the bulletin board - you can be assured that you are influencing that moment of decision when an employee is faced with the choice-to steal or not to steal.

Haphazard Physical Security

Also high on the list of invitations to theft is haphazard physical security. Owner-managers who are casual about issuing keys, locking doors, and changing locks are, in effect, inviting the dishonest employee into the plant or office after work. But intelligent key control and installation of timelocks and alarms are ways of serving notice to crooked workers to play it straight.

Sometimes profits go out the window - literally. For example, one distributor caught "trusted" employees lowering TV sets and tape recorders from a third-story warehouse window to confederates below. Unfortunately they were not caught until they had milked their boss of thousands of dollars worth of merchandise.

But more often, the industrial thief uses a door rather than a window. And the more doors a plant has, the more avenues of theft it offers.

The plant that's designed for maximum security will have a minimum number of active doors and a supervisor or guard, if warranted, stationed near each door. Moreover, a supervisor should be present when materials or finished goods are being received or shipped and when trash is being removed. As long as a door stays open, a responsible employee, a supervisor, or a guard should be there.

Central station alarm systems should be used to protect a plant after hours. Their purpose is to record door openings and closings and to investigate unexpected openings. Timelocks are also designed to record all openings.

"Breaking-out"

A record of door openings can be important because the dishonest employee is often a specialist at "breaking out" (hiding and leaving the plant after closing hours). If your plant is not protected against break-out, you can be hurt badly because this method of operation allows a thief to work pretty much at his or her own speed.

After-hours thieves put out of commission the alarm system that works beautifully against break-in. They can often leave by doors equipped with snap-type locks-doors that do not require keys from the insides. Quickly and easily, they can pass goods outside and then snap doors closed behind them. Thus, they leave no evidence.

A motion detector, electric eye, or central station alarm will deter such thieves. You can also discourage break-outs with locks that need keys on both sides, provided that fire regulations do not prohibit such locks. When goods, materials, or money are missing and evidence of forced entry is lacking, begin to look immediately for the inside thief, the dishonest employee.

Audit Control Methods

Loss prevention controls and procedures by themselves are not enough to protect your assets. Controls and procedures must be audited from time to time or they will break down. No loss-prevention control is stronger than its audit.

One effective auditing method is to commit deliberate errors. What will your people do if, for example, you see that more finished goods than the shipping order calls for reach the platform? Will the shipping clerk return the excess to stock? Will he or she try to divert it for personal use (perhaps in collusion with a truck driver)? Or will the clerk simply ship the order without ever knowing that the excess existed?

If the bookkeeper and the accounts receivable clerk are not dependable, alert, and honest, disaster can result. Check them by withholding an invoice from each of them and watching to see what they do. Will they miss the invoice? Will they realize that a missing invoice means lost revenue and call it to your attention?

Unannounced inspections are another excellent method of checking your preventive procedures. Such inspections are most effective during overtime periods or when the second or third shift is working. For example, one owner-manager popped up on the shipping platform after the second shift left. He noticed a loaded truck parked at the platform and ordered it unloaded. The cartons in the rear were legitimate deliveries, but he found the front half of the truck crammed with stolen goods. The checker, who was hired to see that such stealing did not happen, had gone to sleep and let the accommodating driver load his own truck.

Influence Employees

You should never underestimate your ability to influence your employees in the direction of honesty. Your use of good controls, stiff loss-prevention procedures, and cleverly located physical security devices are powerful reminders to employees that the boss does indeed care.

But controls and devices can be wasted if the owner-manager fails to set a personal example of honesty and conscientiousness. A personal example of high integrity by the boss is the most important step in demonstrating to employees that dishonesty is intolerable.

Such an example includes following the same loss prevention rules that apply to employees. For instance, the owner-manager should sign for items he or she takes from the stockroom just like any other person.

Keep Crooks Off Balance

The crooked employees who are the most successful at their "second trade" are the ones who test the system and are convinced that they can beat it. They can steal you blind. With every "score," their confidence increases and along with it their danger to the company. The best way to stop such crooks is to keep them off balance - keep them from developing the feeling that they can beat your system.

Here's an example of how one owner-manager keeps crooks off balance. When inventory shrinkage became a major problem, he made a loss-prevention survey. To help keep employees honest, he tightened certain existing controls and put in some new ones. He reduced the number of exits employees could use by half. He scheduled "unscheduled" locker inspections for the unlikeliest possible moments. Employees were no longer allowed to take lunch boxes or bags of any kind to their work stations. Package inspection procedures were tightened.

To date, this owner-manager has caught no thieves. But by simply tightening controls and adding a number of surprise elements to his loss-prevention maintenance system, he reduced his inventory loss drastically.

Don't Play Detective

Dishonest employees, working alone or in collusion with others, can find ways to beat the system no matter how theft-proof you try to make it. "Smart cookies" can devise ways to get away with substantial amounts of money, materials, or goods.

Owner-managers who suspect theft should not attempt to turn detective and try to solve the crimes themselves.

Even the best business owner may botch a criminal investigation because it's an area in which the average owner is an amateur.

When you suspect a theft, bring the police or a reliable firm of professional security consultants into the picture without delay. Where dishonest employees are bonded by insurance companies, ironclad evidence of theft must be uncovered before you can file a claim with the insurance company to recover your losses. Professional undercover investigation is among the most effective ways to secure such evidence.

Rules Can Help Reduce Pilferage

Employees who are caught stealing will be prosecuted. (Settling for restitution and an apology is inviting theft to continue.)

Rotate security guards. (Rotation discourages fraternizing with other employees who may turn out to be dishonest. Rotation also prevents monotony from reducing the alertness of guards.)

Never assign two or more members of the same family to work in the same area. (You can expect blood to be thicker than company loyalty.)

Key employees will be kept informed about the activities and findings of the person who is in charge of security. (Thus weak points in security can be strengthened without delay.)

Make a dependable second check of incoming materials to rule out the possibility of collusive theft between drivers and employees who handle the receiving:

No truck shall approach the loading platform until it is ready to load or unload.

Drivers will not be allowed behind the receiving fence. (Discourage drivers from taking goods or materials from the platform by the following devices: heavy-gauge wire fencing between bays, with the mesh too fine to provide a toehold; closed-circuit television cameras, mounted overhead so as to sweep the entire platform; and locating the receiving supervisor's desk or office to afford him or her an unobstructed view of the entire platform.)

At the loading platform, drivers will not be permitted to load their own trucks, especially by taking goods from stock.

Every lunch box, tool box, bag, or package must be inspected by a supervisor or guard as employees leave the plant.

All padlocks must be snapped shut on hasps when not in use to prevent the switching of locks.

Keys to padlocks must be controlled. Never leave the key hanging on a nail near the lock where a crooked worker can "borrow" it and have a duplicate made while he or she is away from work.

Trash must not be allowed to accumulate in, or be picked up from, an area near storage sites of valuable materials or finished goods.

Inspect disposal locations and rubbish trucks at irregular intervals for the presence of salable items when you have the slightest reason to suspect collusion between employees and trash collectors.

Trash pickups must be supervised. (Companies have been systematically drained over long periods by alliance between crooked employees and trash collectors.)

Control receiving reports and shipping orders (preferably by numbers in sequence) to prevent duplication of fraudulent payment of invoices and the padding or destruction of shipping orders.

Receiving reports must be prepared immediately upon receiving a shipment. (Delay in making out such reports can be an invitation to theft or, at best, result in record keeping errors.)

4. How to Outwit Bad-Checks Passers

Time was when a man's word was as good as his bond. But nowadays, even the signatures of many persons are worthless - especially to retailers who are stuck with bad checks and bounced check.

This Chapter offers suggestions that should be helpful in keeping bad checks out of the cash register of stores. For example, the key items on a check should be examined closely because they can tip off the owner-manager to a worthless check. Your procedures should also include a dollar limit on the size of checks you will accept and the type of identification necessary to back up the signature or endorsement. In addition, it is profitable to review with employees the checks which the bank refuses to honor.

A neatly dressed stranger pays for her groceries with a payroll check issued by a company in a nearby city, In the next few hours she does the same thing in several other food stores.

In another community, a middle-aged man pays for a pair of shoes with a Government check. He moves to other stores and cashes several more Government checks.

In another community, a well-dressed woman pays for an expensive dress with a blank check. "I need a little pocket cash," she says. "May I make the check for $20 more?" The salesclerk agrees, never suspecting that the customer does not have an account in any bank.

Tomorrow, these three con-artists will work in other communities.

The specialist in payroll checks will fill out blank ones which she has stolen. The passer of Government checks is also a thief. He steals Social Security checks, tax refund checks, and so on from individual mail boxes. "Blank check" Bessie will hit her victim after the banks have closed.

These three, and others who pass worthless checks, are clever. They live by their wits and are often glib talkers. But they are not so clever that you can't outwit them.

Types of Checks

Winning the battle of wits against **bad-checks / bounced check** passers is largely a matter of knowledge and vigilance. You have to know what you're up against, pass the information on to your employees, and be constantly on guard when accepting checks.

You are apt to get seven different kinds of checks: personal, two-party, payroll. Government, blank, counter, and travelers. And some customers may offer money orders.

A Personal Check is written and signed by the individual offering it. The individual makes it out to you or your firm.

A Two-Party Check is issued by one person, the maker, to a second person who endorses it so that it may be cashed by a third person. This type of check is susceptible to fraud because, for one thing, the maker can stop payment at the bank.

A Payroll Check is issued to an employee for wages or salary earned. Usually the name of the employer is printed on it, and it has a number and is signed. In most instances "payroll" is also printed on the check. The employee's name is printed by a check writing machine or typed. In metropolitan areas, you should not cash a payroll check that is hand written, rubber stamped or typewritten as a payroll check, even if it appears to be issued by a local business and drawn on a local bank. It may be a different story in a small community where you know the company officials and the employee personally.

A Government Check can be issued by the Federal Government, a State, a county, or a local government. Such checks cover salaries, tax refunds, pensions, welfare allotments, and veterans benefits, to mention a few examples.

You should be particularly cautious with government checks. Often they are stolen and the endorsement has been forged.

In some areas, such thievery is so great that some banks refuse to cash Social Security, welfare, relief, or income tax checks, unless the customer has an account with the bank. You should follow this procedure also. In short, know your endorser.

A Blank Check, sometimes known as a universal check, is not longer acceptable to most banks due to the Federal Reserve Board regulations that prohibit standard processing without the encoded characters. This universal check may be used, but it requires a special collection process by the bank and incurs a special cost.

A Counter Check is still used by a few banks and is issued to depositors when they are withdrawing funds from their accounts. It is not good anywhere else. Sometimes a store has its own counter checks for the convenience of its customers. A counter check is not negotiable and is so marked.

A Traveler's Check is a check sold with a preprinted amount (usually in round figures) to travelers who do not want to carry large amounts of cash. The traveler signs the checks at the time of purchase and should counter-sign the check only in the presence of the person who cashes them.

In addition, a Money Order can be passed as a check. However, a money order is usually sent in the mail. Most stores should not accept money orders in face-to-face transactions.

Some small stores sell money orders, If yours does, never accept a personal check in payment for money orders. If the purchaser has a valid checking account, why does he or she need a money order? The check is possible no good.

Look For Key Items

A check carries several key items such as name and location of bank, date, amount (in figures and spelled out), and signature. Close examination of such key items can sometimes tip you off to a worthless check. Before accepting a check, look for:

Nonlocal Banks. Use extra care in examining a check that is drawn on a nonlocal bank and require positive identification. List the customer's local and out-of-town address and phone number on the back of the check.

Date. Examine the date for accuracy of day, month, and year. Do not accept the check if it's postdated, or if it's more than 30 days old.

Location. Look first to be sure that the check shows the name, branch, town, and State where the bank is located.

Amount. Be sure that the numerical amount agrees with the written amount.

Legibility. Do not accept a check that is not written legibly. It should be written and signed in ink and must not have any erasures or written-over amounts.

Payee. When you take a personal check on your selling floor, have the customer make it payable to our firm. Special care should be used in taking a two-party check.

Amount of Purchase. Personal checks should be for the exact amount of the purchase. The customer should receive no change.

Checks Over Your Limit. Set a limit on the amount - depending on the amount of your average sale - you will accept on a check. When a customer wants to go beyond that limit, your salesclerk should refer the customer to you.

Low Sequence Numbers. Be more cautious with low sequence numbers. Experience indicates that there seems to be a higher number of these checks that are returned. Most banks who issue personalized checks begin the numbering system with 101 and numbering sequence when a customer reorders new checks.

Amount of Check. Most bad-check passers pass checks in the $25.00 to $35.00 range on the assumption that the retailer will be more cautious when accepting a larger check.

Types of Merchandise Purchased. Be watchful of the types of merchandise purchased. Random sizes, selections, lack of concern about prices by customers should indicate to you that a little more caution should be exercised when a check is offered as payment.

Require Identification

Once you are satisfied that the check is okay, the question is, "Is the person holding the check the right person?" Requiring identification helps you to answer the question.

But keep in mind that no identification is foolproof. A crook is a crook no matter what type of identification you ask to see. If the person wants to forge identification, he or she can.

Some stores demand at least two pieces of identification. It is important to get enough identification so the person presenting the check can be identified and located if and when the check turns out to be worthless.

The following types of identification should be useful in determining the type to use in your store.

Current Automobile Operators License. If licenses in your State do not carry a photograph of the customer, you may want to ask for a second identification.

Automobile Registration Card. Be sure the name of the State agrees with the location of the bank. If it doesn't, the customer should be able to explain why they don't agree. Also make sure that the signatures on the registration and check agree.

Shopping Plates, If they bear a signature or laminated photograph, shopping plates or other credit cards can be used as identification. The retail merchants' organization in some communities issues lists of stolen shopping plates to which you should always refer when identifying the check passer.

Government Passes can also be used for identification in cashing checks. Picture passes should carry the name of the employing department and a serial number. Building passes should also carry a signature.

Identification Cards, such as those issued by the armed services, police departments, and companies, should carry a photo, a description, and a signature. Police cards should also carry a badge number.

Several types of cards and documents are not good identification. Some of them (for example, club cards) are easily forged, and others (for example, customer's duplicate sales-checks) were never intended for identification. Unless they are presented with a current automobile operator's license, do not accept the following:

Social Security Cards

Letters

Business Cards

Birth Certificates

Club or Organization Cards

Library Cards

Bank Books

Initialed Jewelry

Work Permits

Unsigned Credit Cards

Insurance Cards

Voter's Registration Cards

Learner's Permits

Customer's Duplicate Cards

Some large stores photograph each person who cashes a check along with the identification. This procedure is a deterrent because bad-check passers don't want to be photographed.

Some stores, when in doubt about a check, will verify an address and telephone number in the local telephone directory or with the information operator. Someone intending to pass a bad check will not necessarily be at the address shown on the check. If the address and telephone number cannot be verified, the check should be considered a potentially bad check.

Compare Signatures

Regardless of the type of identification you require, it is essential that you and your employees compare the signature on the check with the one on the identification.

You should also compare the person standing before you with the photograph and or description on the identification.

Set A Policy

You should set a policy for cashing checks, write it down, and instruct your employees in its use. Your policy might require your approval before a salesclerk can cash a check. When all checks are handled alike, customers have no cause to feel that they are being treated unfairly.

Your procedure might include the use of a rubber stamp. Many stores stamp the lower reverse side of a check and write in the appropriate information. Your policy might also include verifying a check through the bank that issued the check. Some banks will do this only if you are a depositor in the bank. It might be helpful to establish business accounts in several banks, particularly where many of your customers have accounts.

You may want to verify a check through a check verification service. Should you contract with such a service or if you receive lists of bad-check passers, ask the service to show you proof from the Federal Trade Commission that their service is in compliance with the Fair Credit Reporting Act.

Employee apathy toward accepting checks is a big reason why stores get stuck with bad checks. The bigger the store, the more difficult is to keep employees interested in catching bad checks. One effective way is to show employees your bad checks.

Refusing A Check

Review your policy and procedure on check cashing frequently with your employees. Remind them of what to look for to spot bad checks.

You are not obligated to take anyone's check. Even when a stranger presents satisfactory identification, you do not have to accept the check.

In most cases, you accept a check when the customer has met your identification requirements. You want to make the sale. But never accept a check if the person presenting it appears to intoxicated.

Never take a check if the customer acts suspiciously. For example, the customer may try to rush you or your employees while you are checking identification.

Never take a check that is dated in advance.

Never discriminate when refusing a check. Don't tell a customer that you can't accept a check because he or she is a college student or lives in a bad neighborhood, etc. If you do, you may be in violation of a State or Federal law on discrimination.

What Can You Recover?

Whether or not you recover any money lost on a bad check depends on the person who gave it to you. He or she may be one of your best customers who inadvertently gave you a check when the funds in his or her bank account were insufficient. On the other end of the scale, he or she may be a forger.

Once you are stuck with a bad check, here are some of the situations you face.

Insufficient Funds. Most checks returned because of insufficient funds clear the second time you deposit them. Notify the customer that his or her account is overdrawn and that you are redepositing the check. But if the check is returned a second time, in some localities, it is the retailer's collection problem and you must try to get the maker to honor the check by paying immediately.

You should check the practices of your bank. In some areas, for example, after a second return for insufficient funds, the bank will not let you re-deposit the check. It is your collection problem. Some stores prosecute if the customer does not redeem such a check within a week of the second return. Stores with a reputation for being easy-going about insufficient funds checks usually get plenty of them.

The procedure for prosecution depends on the State. In one jurisdiction, for example, a merchant must send the check writer a certified or registered notice of an intention to prosecute. The bad-check writer then has five days from date of receipt of that notice to comply before the merchant can prosecute. In another jurisdiction, the maker has five days after the date of notice to make the check good. In a third, a resident has ten days to make good on the check.

No Account. Usually you've lost when the bank returns a check marked "no account." Such a check is evidence of a swindle or a fraud unless there has been an extraordinary error. In rare instances, a customer may issue a check on the wrong bank or on a discontinued account. You should quickly determine what the circumstances are. If the person is known in the community, proceed with your collection efforts. If you find yourself "stuck" with the check, call your police department.

Closed Account. A check marked "closed account" is a warning of extreme carelessness or fraud. Accounts are closed by both individuals and by banks. The latter may close an account because of too many overdrafts. An individual may open a new account by removing funds from an old account. In such case, the individual may forget that he or she has issued a check that is still outstanding against the old account.

If you don't get your money back within a reasonable time, you should consider prosecuting the check writer.

Forgery. Forged checks are worthless - a total loss to you.

Watch out for smudged checks, misspelled words, poor spacing of letters or numbers indicating that changes may have been made. Payroll checks with the company's name and address typed in could be fraudulent. Most payroll checks are printed.

When you suspect forgery, call the police. Thus, you can help yourself and others against further forgery. Refer a U.S. Government check to the field office of the U.S. Secret Service.

Check with your lawyer about court collection practices in your area. In the Washington, D.C. area, for example, merchants cannot collect through the courts on bad checks used to pay on an open account. The reason is: The merchant still has the account and no injury was suffered through the issuance of the check. The account may be collectable through the usual civil procedures used for collection purposes.

Any alteration, illegal signature(s) of the maker of the check, a forgery of the endorsement, an erasure or an obliteration on a genuine check is a crime.

A bad check issued to pay for merchandise is not a theft but a misdemeanor. It is an exchange - the checks for goods. A misdemeanor carries a lighter penalty than a theft since a check may be collectable through civil procedures. Criminal action may be taken through signing a formal charge with the police.

Get Evidence. You cannot prosecute bad-check passers without good evidence. The person who cashed the bad check should be positively identified and connected with the receiving of money for it.